Sea Turtles Past and Present

Marianne Johnston

The Rosen Publishing Group's
PowerKids Press™
New York

Published in 2000 by The Rosen Publishing Group, Inc.
29 East 21st Street, New York, NY 10010

First Edition

Book Design: Michael deGuzman, Resa Listort, Danielle Primiceri

Photo Credits: p. 3 © Tom Brakefield/Corbis; p. 4 © David Fleetham/FPG International; pp. 6–7 © American Museum of Natural History; p. 8 © Brandon D. Cole/Corbis and © American Museum of Natural History; p. 10 © Beach Hills Museum; p. 12 © Stephen Fink/Corbis; p. 14 © Clem Haagner; ABPL/Corbis; p. 15 © Galen Rowell/Corbis; p. 16 © George H. H. Huey/Animals Animals; p. 17 © Ken G. Preston-Matham/Animals Animals; p. 18 © Lynda Richardson/Corbis; p. 19 © Kennan Ward/Corbis; p. 20 © Rick Doyle/Corbis. pp. 21–22 © Digital Stock 1995, Beach Hills Museum.

Johnston, Marianne.
    Sea Turtles Past and Present / by Marianne Johnston.
        p.   cm. — (Prehistoric animals and their modern-day relatives)
    Includes index.
    Summary: Discusses the prehistoric ancestors, evolution, modern species, life cycle, and endangered status of sea turtles.
    ISBN 0-8239-5205-3
    1. Sea Turtles—Juvenile literature. [1. Sea Turtles. 2. Turtles. 3. Endangered species. 4. Prehistoric animals.]
  I. Title. II. Series.
    QL666.C536J64   1998   97-52010
    597.92—dc21   CIP
                                                   AC

Manufactured in the United States of America

CONTENTS

TIME TRAVELERS

Today, at least seven **species** of sea turtles swim the waters from the Atlantic Ocean to the Pacific Ocean to the Mediterranean Sea. Sea turtles have been gliding through the waters of Earth for millions of years. The most amazing thing about sea turtles is that, unlike most living things, sea turtles have hardly changed in 200 million years! The biggest change for the earliest relative of the sea turtle was where it lived. It changed its **habitat** from land to sea.

Sea turtles are **reptiles**. Even though they live in the ocean, they swim to the **surface** often to get air.

◀ *Sea turtles glide through the water like birds glide through the air.*

The **ancestors** of all of today's turtles started out on land. The oldest **prehistoric** turtle was **Proganochelys** who lived about 220 million years ago.

This turtle was three feet long and had small horns on the back of its neck.

Proganochelys had very few teeth, and probably ate plants that grew along the ground.

Some land turtles, like Proganochelys, began to **adapt** to life in the sea. Over millions of years, their feet and legs slowly developed into flippers.

Proganochelys used the horns on its neck for extra protection.

WHY ARE SEA TURTLES SPECIAL?

Unlike other turtles, sea turtles spend all of their time in the water, except when laying their eggs. Instead of having feet, like other turtles, sea turtles have powerful flippers. A sea turtle's shell is flatter than the shells of other kinds of turtles. This allows the sea turtle to glide more smoothly through the water.

Two **aquatic** prehistoric turtles had the flippers and flat shell, which are **characteristics** of today's sea turtles. These ancient turtles were called **Stupendemys** and **Palaeotrionyx**. Both of these turtles were adapted to life in the water. Instead of living in the ocean, like sea turtles, these two turtles swam in freshwater, such as the Amazon River in South America.

Legs with feet are fine for land turtles, but flippers help sea turtles move more easily underwater.

Archelon: A Giant Sea Turtle

Today's sea turtles are much bigger than many land and freshwater turtles. But even modern-day sea turtles aren't as big as **Archelon** was. Archelon is the only prehistoric sea turtle that we know of so far. Archelon lived in the ocean 70 million years ago.

This giant ancient sea turtle didn't have a hard outer shell like other turtles did. Instead, Archelon's ribs spread out to form its back. Over this frame stretched a thick layer of rubber-like skin. Archelon also had huge paddle-like flippers.

With its flippers and lighter shell, the twelve-foot-long Archelon could move swiftly through the water.

Sea Turtles Today

Five kinds of sea turtles swim in American waters. The loggerhead, Kemp's ridley, green, leatherback, and hawksbill turtles are found on the coasts of Florida, Georgia, North and South Carolina, and Texas.

The leatherback's dark body is spotted with small white spots. Being the largest of the sea turtles, the leatherback can weigh up to 800 pounds. One particular leatherback measured almost ten feet long! This turtle looks a bit like the prehistoric Archelon.

The smallest sea turtles are the Kemp's ridley turtles. These two-foot long, yellow-and-green turtles are the most **endangered** of all the sea turtles.

There are laws in the United States to help protect endangered sea turtle species.

13

THE LOGGERHEAD

Thousands of loggerhead turtles are born every year on the coast of Florida. If you see a turtle laying eggs during a warm summer night on a Florida beach, chances are you're seeing a loggerhead. Florida is not the only place you'll see a loggerhead. These turtles live from Canada all the way down to South America.

These large-headed turtles start life as tiny **hatchlings**. They grow into graceful adults that are three feet long and have reddish-brown shells and yellow bellies. Loggerheads also have strong jaw muscles. They use their strong jaws to crack open the shells of the clams and crabs that they love to eat.

As an adult, this baby loggerhead will have a shell that weighs 150 to 400 pounds. ▶

EGG-LAYING TIME

Scientists believe that when a sea turtle is ready to lay her eggs, she travels back to the exact same beach on which she was born. Sometimes this means swimming thousands of miles.

16

When a female turtle reaches the beach, she pulls herself out of the water and uses her flippers to inch her way up the beach. Then, in a safe spot, the turtle digs a hole in the sand with her back flippers. Next she lays about 100 eggs in the hole. The eggs look like Ping-Pong balls. The mother turtle then fills the hole with sand and heads back to the sea.

Scientists are very interested in this **method** of laying eggs. They believe that sea turtles from long ago laid their eggs in the same way.

◁ *We do not know for sure how female turtles find the beaches where they were born.*

Unfortunately, many turtle eggs are stolen by humans or eaten by animals, such as raccoons, before the eggs are ready to hatch. If the eggs don't get eaten or stolen, the baby turtles hatch after about two months.

Baby turtles use a special tooth on their snout to poke out of their eggs.

Baby turtles almost always hatch during the night. Once out of the egg, the babies scurry out of the nest and toward the sea. Sometimes the moon shining on the water helps baby turtles find the sea.

Sea Turtles and Humans

The oceans of the world were once home to millions of sea turtles. Now there are only a few hundred thousand left. Like many other animals, sea turtles have become endangered because of humans.

Over the years, people have killed turtles for their meat and shells. People have also killed turtles by accident. Trash, such as a plastic sandwich bag, can harm turtles and other sea animals. A sea turtle may think a plastic bag is a jellyfish. If the turtle eats the bag, it could get stuck inside the turtle's body and kill the turtle.

You can help turtles and other sea animals by cleaning up your trash at the beach.

The Sea Turtle: Yesterday and Today

Sea turtles haven't changed very much since creatures like Archelon swam in the ocean. Today's sea turtles have the same flat shell and strong flippers as prehistoric aquatic turtles. And sea turtles today lay their eggs much like their ancestors did.

Many people are working hard to protect today's sea turtles. For example, in many places it is against the law to kill sea turtles or to buy sea turtle parts. Also, fishermen must place a special tool in their nets that allows sea turtles to escape if they are caught. Sea turtles are an important part of animal history. Working together, we can learn about the sea turtle's past and protect its future.

Web Site:

http://www.geocities.com/Heartland/Plains/3550/evolve.html

22

GLOSSARY

adapt (uh-DAPT) To change to fit different conditions.

ancestor (AN-ses-ter) A creature from which others develop.

aquatic (uh-KWAH-tik) Having to do with water.

Archelon (AR-keh-lon) The only known prehistoric sea turtle.

characteristic (KAR-ik-tuh-RIS-tik) A special quality or feature.

endangered (en-DAYN-jerd) When something is in danger of no longer existing.

habitat (HA-bih-tat) The surroundings where an animal lives.

hatchling (HACH-ling) A baby turtle that has just come out of its shell.

method (MEH-thid) A way of doing something.

Palaeotrionyx (puh-LAY-ee-o-tree-on-ix) Prehistoric freshwater turtle with flippers and a flat shell.

prehistoric (pree-his-TOR-ik) Happening before recorded history.

Proganochelys (proh-gan-eh-KEH-lus) The oldest known turtle that lived 220 million years ago.

reptile (REP-tyl) An air-breathing animal that hatches from an egg and lives in a warm area.

species (SPEE-sheez) A group of plants or animals that are very much alike.

Stupendemys (stoo-PEN-duh-mus) A prehistoric freshwater turtle with flippers and a flat shell.

surface (SER-fis) The top or outside of something.

23

INDEX